Post Agile Depression

Weaknesses, Impacts, and Effects When Implementing an Agile Development Model

2ⁿᵈ Edition
Revised and Updated

By
Jonathan Cook

Visit the author's website for more information.
https://sites.google.com/site/jccookauthor/

Contents

Executive Summary

Please note: This Executive Report draws heavily from the author's research published in other more broad based reports. You may wish to review the author's other reports to see if they may provide additional information for your needs.

The Agile development method is in great demand in the modern business world. Although generally thought of as applying to software development, the Agile method can be applied to other types of projects as well. This report will take the perspective of the Agile method relative to software development but it is not limited only to software development.

As wonderful as Agile sounds in the literature supporting it and the oft documented results that a multitude of Agile consultants will display before you, Agile is not without its side effects—not least of which is the impacts on the staff workers themselves.

Implementing an Agile development model upon an existing team or department can have significant short and long term impacts to both the productivity and retention of a team or department. This is not to be considered lightly.

In the decades of experience accumulated by the author it has been seen first hand the positive and negative impacts of the Agile methods as applied to existing functional and productive teams.

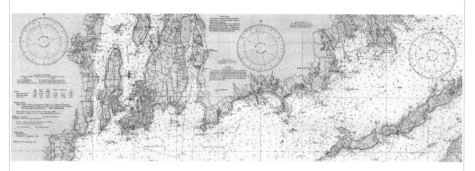

Introduction

Is Agile the right development method for you? If you are already using Agile is it working as promised? Do you know the drawbacks and impacts it may have on your team?

The Agile development method promises to improve your project outcomes dramatically. Depending on which books you read or which consultants you consult, Agile may promise to improve your productivity, reduce your costs, speed your projects to completion, make your staff happy and your customers even happier. In short, depending on your sources, it may promise to rock your world.

However, those promises may not fit the real world. Agile may (or may not) improve your outcomes, but you need to balance possible improved outcomes with unanticipated costs, both financial and, for you and your teams, personal.

This report will help you understand and anticipate the costs of Agile that are rarely talked about or understood. With this information you can improve your current Agile implementation or better prepare your team and processes for the shift to a new Agile implementation.

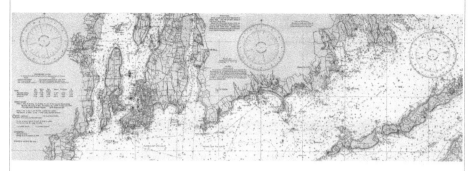

The Agile Development Method

The Agile development method, commonly referred to as simply *Agile,* is a group or mix of development ideologies that stress small steps in the development process such that the product progresses through a series of incremental improvements until a final product is completed and delivered.

A common definition of the Agile model is:

Agile software development is a group of software development methods based on iterative and incremental development, where requirements and solutions evolve through collaboration between self-organizing, cross-functional teams. It promotes adaptive planning, evolutionary development and delivery, a time-boxed iterative approach, and encourages rapid and flexible response to change. It is a conceptual framework that promotes foreseen interactions throughout the development cycle.[1]

In general, the various Agile models have taken on the mantra of best practice in the industry and Agile is being adopted by many development shops precisely because it does promise better results. However, promises and results can quite often be different.

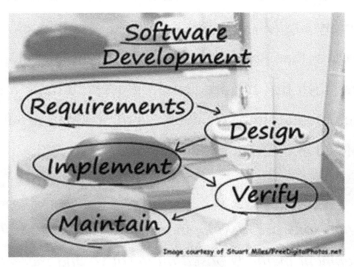

All development methods have both strengths and weaknesses. However, in the real world the weaknesses of Agile are rarely pointed out by the newly hired consultant to the client looking to adopt an Agile process. In essence, all weaknesses are glossed over and attributed

[1] http://en.wikipedia.org/wiki/Agile_software_development

to client mistakes while implementing the consultant's Agile advise.

This Executive Report will not elaborate on the strengths of Agile as these are well documented in the industry literature. Rather this report will point out weaknesses that need to be considered by the reader when adopting a new Agile development method.

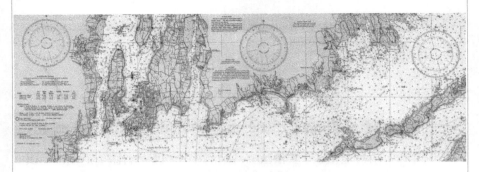

Common Agile Weaknesses

Like it or not Agile does have weaknesses. It is these weaknesses, when overlooked, that create what the author likes to term "Post Agile Depression". This is not simply a play on words. With decades of software development experience in many industries and under a number of methods, the author has seen first hand the impacts on the moral of teams in environments that did not account for these Agile weaknesses.

Agile environments should consider the following weaknesses when implementing Agile.

Poor Documentation

One of the primary tenets of Agile is reduced documentation. Code should be self documenting (with few if any comments) and project documentation is held to a minimum. This generally results in poor communications, poor historical project knowledge and project confusion between the various elements of the overall team. Waterfall may have too much documentation but that is not an excuse to have too little documentation. This problem often relates directly to the other weakness listed in this section.

Poor Customer/Client Involvement

Ideally, domain knowledgeable customer representatives are part of the Agile development team, spending significant time side-by-side with the developers and QA representatives as the product is being developed. Business reality rarely allows this. The customers with the best domain knowledge are in great demand by many areas of their business and rarely have time to spend with the developers. Customers who may have time generally do not have the required domain knowledge. For large projects in large organizations this can be particularly difficult as many domains may need to be a part of the project.

The end result is poor customer involvement and relations. The author has observed a number of situations, in large organization, where the customer is not even aware that a project is in progress just when they are required to get involved in the development process. As such, development stalls and resources are left idle.

Poor Project Interface Management

In today's modern and large projects a system is not developed in a vacuum. Rarely is a software system developed that just connects to a local database or

presents a static web page. Large businesses interface with many different systems, each with its own interface requirements. This common situation almost always conflicts with the ideals of Agile. Connecting to a local database may sound simple and easy to accomplish within an Agile sprint, but if the database team is not on-board with the Agile process, they may not meet the Sprint's goals or their design requirements may even conflict with the general project design. Furthermore, necessary Web Services may not exists and Security departments may refuse network access or impose cumbersome connection requirements.

The common solution is to mock the various interfaces such that the rest of development can proceed. This works for a short time, but there comes a point when the real interface is required. In addition, the mock interface rarely accounts for all of the nuances of the real interface.

Poor Time Management

Agile promises that team members, overworked by other development processes, will now work in an environment free from extraneous distractions with clearly defined goals contained in well defined time sprints. The work will be less stressful and more sustainable.

The author has yet to observe this. The common

reality of business is such that developers are often pulled aside to attend to issues of legacy software, other projects running in parallel with the primary project and a myriad of HR and other non-project related tasks. Just recording project metrics, as often demanded by management, can result in significant loss of productive time.

In addition, project managers, intent on making sure their project plans look good, rarely buffer for vacation and sick time off. Many can't even properly resource an FTE (Full Time Equivalent) resource.

Poor Quality Assurance (QA) Involvement

This is similar to poor customer/client involvement. Good QA practices state that the people testing a system should not be the same people developing the system (similar to Separation of Duties in Generally Accepted Accounting Principals). As such, the QA team has to schedule their involvement with the Agile practice much the same way as the customer. This can result in similar problems.

Pairing is Counterproductive

Developer pairing is one of the primary goals of Agile. Pairing is designed to encourage ongoing code reviews; faster, more productive coding sessions (cleaner code through continuous re-factoring); cross training of the developers (as stronger developers naturally teach weaker developers) and training to the code set, as the developers are exposed to more of the project code.

Image courtesy of Renjith Krishnan/FreeDigitalPhotos.net

Unfortunately, the author has not observed these results in real practice. The reality of pairing often results in:

Personality conflicts

These include the typical interpersonal issues that strongly creative people face when working close together, and stronger developers are hindered and annoyed by weaker developers.

Resources are idle

Even with the proper tools, only one person can type code at a time. This leaves one developer idle. This may be the stated goal of Agile as the idle developer can observe the working developer and catch any errors. See personality conflicts.

Remote issues

In today's world developers are often remotely located and work over the wire. This can create additional issues.

If the business customer/client resource is also not remotely available then the developer pair may be idle.

Pair schedule conflicts

This may be as simple as bathroom and lunch breaks to as complex as vacation and other time-off conflicts. Agile states that any one person can pair with any other person at any time, but this rarely works well in practice per the other listed issues. In addition, people naturally work at different paces and conflicting paces will stress one and bore another.

A few good developers end up doing all of the work

This is particularly vexing as strong developers tend to do the bulk of the work. Ideally, the weak developers will become strong developers, but as is often the case the strong developers just dominate and the weak developers get frustrated.

Lack of privacy

Working in pairs in a large development room leaves little privacy and private space. Humans are naturally social, but also private. Both of these are stressed when people are *forced* into group (and pairing) situations.

Lack of ownership and responsibility

Agile states that developers should not own their code and that everyone is responsible for all of the code. This sounds ideal, but much like socialism it often results in no-one taking responsibility for code and bug fixes.

Teams are too Big and Hard to Manage

Agile teams can be large or small depending on available resources and team design, however they are generally a minimum of four to six people. A project may consist of several teams and these may cross-matrix with multiple other teams from other departments which may in turn matrix with other departments. A spider web of interaction can occur which creates management conflicts (project and personnel).

This can be a problem with any development model, but Agile's loosely coupled, self-organizing, cross-functional team model can aggravate standard management practices as the process conflicts with org charts and established authority pathways.

Sprints are too Short/too Much Work

This is similar to poor time management but is directly related to Sprint duration. Sprints must allow for all of the elements required.

Project Scope Expansion

This is essentially the same scope issue found in other

development models. However, Agile's loosely coupled, self-organizing, cross-functional team model can aggravate this as different teams accept new scope requests independent of other teams and without a central coordination process.

Incomplete Projects

Agile's goal is to balance Scope, Resources and Time. A lack of resources means that scope must be reduced or time extended. Similarly, a lack of time means more

Image courtesy of Stuart Miles/FreeDigitalPhotos.net

resources and/or less scope. This equation can play out in multiple ways such that the balance should result in a completed project. However, in reality, the result may be an effectively incomplete project. In this case a phase two of the project is usually started and work continues.

Ideally, if all parties agree to all balancing of the equation then an acceptable (though not necessarily ideal) project outcome is the result.

Business Reality Rarely Cooperates

Rarely can business just expand resources and/or time. As such, scope is usually adjusted resulting in a poor skeleton of the original project. Multiple releases of the project then follow and eventually a real product emerges. However, with all of the other issues listed, the entire process may result in a miserable project experience and little enthusiasm for the next project.

Focus Evolves to the Code Quality Rather than to the Results

Whether we like it or not, all that really matters to the customer is a working product, delivered on-time and on-budget. However, Agile's strong emphasis on code quality and re-factoring tends to encourage the team to focus more on the nuances of code quality then on actual results. From an artistic and craft perspective this sounds ideal, but from a business perspective it can hinder progress and result in poor outcomes. Business cares only that code WORKS and solves the problem at hand. It does not care how nuanced the code is. Code should not be flawed from a functional perspective, but it does not need to be perfect from an artistic or engineering perspective.

Many would argue that high quality, self-documenting code allows for better code maintenance and enhancements. Rarely is this actually realized in the real world. Any code later reviewed and modified by the original developer will already be understood by that developer (although very old code is often forgotten even by the original developer) and a new developer will still have to mentally reverse-engineer even the best of code. This is further aggravated by Agile's insistence on reduced documentation and minimal code comments.

The Author's Perspective on Software Development

Software development is NOT a process discipline. It is an art, a craft and a practice. It is emphasized in this and the author's other Executive Reports that software development should not be seen as a factory floor solution, but as a creative solution.

As such, none of the current software development models truly satisfies this reality. One can argue that Agile best fits this reality but in common practice this is not true. In fact, Waterfall even with its structured design, can often better satisfy the *software as art* paradigm.

The author's decades of experience has taught that in order to drive quality outcomes and produce excellent results, the developer resources must be thought of as artists and not as bodies. Developers are not just organization chart entries. They must be seen as creative assets rather than numbers.

This may seem like an obvious conclusion and one that has been touted in management journals for decades. However, when rubber-meets-the-road and metrics do not align with goals, often the first hatchet blows fall upon the heads of the very artists that are the solution, not the problem.

For example, how many times has a project fallen behind in the schedule and the first response is to drive the developers (and other people) into overdrive, demanding more work in less time, cutting vacations, working overtime, etc.? Does this work? It may produce some results for a short time, but constant pressure of this type will actually reduce results.

Or—new resources are hired and added to the teams with the expectation that more people will produce more results. This also tends to fail to produce the expected outcome if for no other reason then the current resources are pulled from real work in order to bring the new hires up to speed with the project. It can take months for a new resource to be truly effective in a new environment.

As you will see below, there are better solutions.

The Developer as Artist and Development as Craft.

It has been emphasized in this report that the developer is an artists and not just a technical resource. Of course there are many arguments against considering developers as artists and the author does not take the perspective that software is always art or that the developer is only an artist.

And many would argue that because software development is technical in nature, it must be science and engineering, not art. Thus, only strict process and organization can produce good results.

The truth lies somewhere in between and each business environment will have its own nuances that make it a unique environment. Only you can know the exact environment in which you work and/or manage. You need to make the final decisions on implementing your model and process.

Given that, the author takes the perspective that software development is an art and a craft. The artistic perspective states that it is a creative process that requires imagination converted into results. The craft perspective states that it can be defined within a process that actually does convert the imagination into results. Both work together to take an idea (requirement) and convert it into a result (solution).

Image courtesy of Adonri/FreeDigitalPhotos.net

There are, of course, many articles and books on how to translate the creative process into real solutions (in any field). However, for the software development process there are a number of concrete elements and steps, rarely addressed, that will be covered in this report. More on this to follow, but quickly, they include:

Clearly define your team and the individual's roles: In the real world individuals (and especially software developers) are pressed to do more for less. This can be counterproductive.

Let your team members be experts in their fields: You will get better results from experts than generalists.

More resources (developers) do not translate to better results.

Retain your talent: Make them want to stay with your organization.

Promote and promote from within.

When you do recruit, hire local talent: They will be more dedicated.

Hire resources proficient in the language of your site and business: If your site works in English be sure everyone speaks English well.

Do not use short term contractors.

Interview recruits in person: At the very least do this at the end of the interview process. Many a recruit has sounded wonderfully competent on the phone simply because they Googled the answers during the phone interview.

Do not hire out of schedule desperation: Give yourself time to find the right people. Then KEEP them.

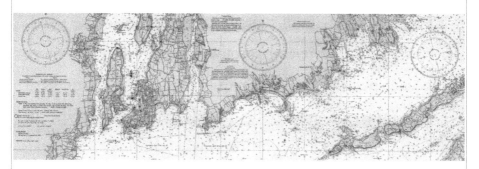

The Author Recommends a New Way to Look at Teams.

Teams cannot be completely free to self-organize as artists tend to be too independent. However, your resources are experts in their field and can certainly

Image courtesy of Renjith Krishnan/FreeDigitalPhotos.net

collaborate on a project. As such, the team needs to be organized using a happy medium of independence and management guidance.

Project specifications should drive the resource needs of the team. Waterfall projects tend to have more involved specifications than Agile projects. Regardless, it is recommended that both models have some type of formal written specifications. Formal written specifications are the driver for resource planning.

Once a project is selected for development the department members (usually a super-set of the eventual project development team) should quickly meet to hash out high level HR and tools resource requirements. Since your resources are experts, this should take little more than half an hour. You are looking for high level input. For example—will the project involve database resources, mid-tier development, client development, what languages, etc.

These types of questions will define the expertise required and thus the general resources and tools required. You can quickly allocate a requirements spec review team to further refine the resources required for the project.

Caution: Do NOT assume that your expert resources

have the time to take on even this early level of effort for a new project! Be sure to allocate the time required in relation to other on-going efforts. Consult with your project manager(s) and the expert resources to make this determination. Assume that they will not have time and be cautious even if they tell you they have time. Artists as expert resources will almost always want to discover the next project and please the boss. It is in their nature as artists to *display* their work.

Fewer Smarter People

Many organizations, managers and the project managers have a tendency to push for more resources in the mistaken believe that more resources will complete a project faster and better than fewer resources. Resources should be allocated to the actual requirements of the project and not to either the available resources (which may be plenty in a large organization) or a perceived tight time line.

This may sound counter-intuitive, but in the development paradigm of developer as artist and process as craft, a smaller number of artist developers can often *ditch digger one day to dig one yard of the ditch. Thus one ditch digger can complete the ditch in 100 days. The project planner mathematically assumes that five diggers can complete the ditch in 20 days and ten diggers can complete it in 10 days. Well, if that is the case then 100 diggers can complete it in one day and 200 diggers can complete it by lunch!*

However, what the project planner fails to realize is the diminishing returns of too many ditch diggers. At some point there will be so many ditch diggers that they will beat themselves silly with so many swinging shovels and so much flying dirt. The diggers get in the way of each other and slow down the progress of the ditch. It is an art, combined with logic that can best determine the optimum number of ditch diggers.

Such is the art and logic of planning a software development project. You just cannot add more resources and expect mathematically increased project progress. There will be too many hypothetical diggers, shovels and loads of dirt. This is generally represented in cross-training efforts and bug fixes imposed on the experienced developers as they try and bring new resources up to speed on the project. You actually slow down the progress of a project rather than speed it up (this also applies to projects in which even experience resources are continually shifted from one project task to another).

The author recommends that you assign and train to a project fewer, smarter, local, non-contract resources rather than simply more resources.

Fewer Resources

This is important as described in the ditch digger analogy. You do not want them stepping on each other or standing idle waiting for work. In addition, fewer resources allows your team to become experts in the project subject matter as well as the tools used to build the project. When a resource is truly working at full capacity on a project they should be able to work in such a way as to rarely consult a technical manual, and rarely require a spec review. In other words, they are fully tuned into the project and can work at full speed.

A resource in this mode is not only more effective for

Local Resources

Local does not mean in the same town or office as resources can be efficient regardless of physical location (albeit time zone differences can create some difficulties). As such, this is misunderstood in today's management paradigm (in addition, the politically correct push for diversity can directly impact this recommendation). Instead, local means cultural and language local. For a team to be at peak effectiveness it should not have to deal with language and cultural barriers. And simply working in the same language does not necessarily mean that everyone understands the same words in the same way. Accents and the cultural use of words can create difficulties in expressing and understanding thoughts and meanings. The author has seen this create major impacts and delays to projects. As such, the common language should be a localized version as much as possible.

In addition, the author has seen language and cultural barriers create interpersonal misunderstandings such that one persons compliment is another's insult. One persons innocent curiosity is another's horrid affront. This can create significant barriers to a team as once these lines are crossed, good relations are hard to recover.

This has nothing to do with nationality, race, religion, etc. It has to do with language skills and cultural experience. Anybody can have these skill sets. It is up to you to hire those that do.

Non-Contract Resources

There is a big temptation in management to hire temporary workers in today's global economic times. The author recommends that you do not hire temporary workers. Instead hire fewer full time workers per the previous reasoning.

The author has met, interviewed and worked with a wide variety of contract resources and these temporary workers can meet the recommended attributes as already discussed. However, on average you will have to weed through more candidates in order to find the few that meet the recommended attributes and, more importantly, you will likely lose these contracted resources at just about the time that they become fully effective with both the required business and technical domain knowledge in your projects.

In theory you can hire the contract resources at the end of their contract, but this can be problematic in larger organizations with less flexible HR rules, and done improperly you can run afoul of the IRS. In addition, contract resources are already familiar with changing jobs and locations and are often more than willing to leave your organization for the next one. In fact, some are in their contracting role specifically for the opportunity to travel to, and work in, a variety of locations.

Contract resources tend to be less vested in your organization and project as they know from the beginning that they are temporary. This is not to say that your full time hires are going to be perfect, but your chances are better.

On paper, contract resources can appear to be less expensive then permanent resources but generally, in the long run, the cost of continually replacing resources as their contract expire (and losing the investment in training, business and project domain knowledge) is more than the cost of the permanent resource.

Another factor to consider is that the contractor may

take valuable inside information to a competitor.

Plan to Train

In today's world management expects that every IT resource knows everything from the first day. Resumes are regularly padded with every acronym and keyword in the industry in hopes of triggering interviews from head-hunter search engines. The author has yet to meet anyone

Image courtesy of Renjith Krishnan/FreeDigitalPhotos.net

who really knows everything listed on their resumes. At best they have been exposed to the items and they are expert in a few key items, at worst they Google these items during the phone interviews in order to sound good to the interviewer (The author has experienced this not-so-subtle technique multiple times).

As such, plan to allow the resources you do hire the time to train on any tools and techniques needed to meet the project requirements. Do not assume that your resources know everything. However, if you have good resources, they can learn rapidly and on their own, given the time.

It is not always necessary to train in a formal classroom setting. In fact this can often be less effective to the artist developer that learns more from curiosity and exploration. Each situation and resource can be different so try and adapt as needed.

Analysts, Developers, Quality Assurance (QA), Project Managers, Trainers, Support, Management

This section will not describe the roles of the team members as this is generally well understood. However, there are unique attributes to these roles that are often overlooked or poorly used in today's organizations.

Each of the development methods in use in today's organizations utilizes some variation of the listed roles and their interrelationships. Much of this has already been discussed here or in other literature. As such, this section will highlight these overlooked elements of each of these roles.

Analysts (often referred to as a Subject Matter Expert (SME) or Systems Analyst)

A good analyst has a broad domain knowledge in some or all of the project (depending on the project size) and good relations with the business and management teams. They can be a good resource between the client, the developers and the rest of the team. However, analysts are often used to create the initial specs, and maybe a few other project definitions, than they are sent off to work on another project, drawn back to the original project only when there is a misunderstanding (and often too late).

While analysts are generally not managers, they can be good coordinators. One key role often overlooked is their ability to see the big picture that encompasses the project design and the developer's tasks. Regardless of the development method employed, a developer will only work on a small snippet of the project at any one time. The analyst is in the best position to see how this fits into the overall project. Most importantly the analyst can feed the developer critical design elements that allow the developer to focus on implementing the design element rather than attempting to see the whole project as the analyst does.

For example, one of the best project development processes the author has seen was utilized such that the developers created a middleware code model of highly repeatable module design patterns (not reusable as each module performed different tasks) working through standardized interfaces to all other elements connected to the middleware. We will call this the Widgets project.

In the Widgets project all design elements passed data via the method signatures defined in the interfaces. Each method had one or more (overloaded) signatures defined such that all inputs and (returned) outputs to/from the middleware were well defined (this may sound obvious, but is actually rarely implemented in a planned, structured, repeatable fashion).

The Widgets project took advantage of the analysts knowledge of the whole project such that the analyst pre-defined the methods and their signatures because the analyst knew, from a high level, the data that needed to move back and forth for each of the required processes of the project. The analyst did not code, but rather defined the interface. The developer could then use the highly repeatable module design pattern to code to the requirements of the method signature. The developer did not need to understand the whole project, only the method signatures provided.

All aspects of the Widgets project worked this way such that developers only coded to the interfaces in and out of their modules. The database experts followed the same routine focusing on their knowledge domain as did the client developers.

It was not unusual for significant new functionality to be defined, coded and integrated into the Widgets project development build in a matter of minutes or hours rather than days. Few bugs occurred and the project was completed before the deadline and under budget. Business was fully satisfied with the results and the system eventually went nationwide for that organization.

The Widgets project required one analyst, two (force

paired) client developers, two (force paired) middleware developers and one database developer. Eventually it was realized that the paired client and middleware teams were less effective working as pairs than as individuals. The pairs broke up and development accelerated.

Developers

Much of this report has focused on the developers of a project. The overlooked roles of a developer have more to do with what a developer is NOT rather than what is a developer.

A developer is not a trainer. A developer is not a tester (QA). A developer is not a project manager or a general manager. A developer may be a lead developer, but unless that lead developer is specifically given domain HR authority, do not ask the developer to manage people in an HR capacity.

Above all, a developer is not a primary support person!

If you want a developer then let the developer develop.

Of course, every business is different in size and

requirements. The members of a small team may naturally have to take on multiple roles in order to complete a project. However, each team resource should know their primary role and their primary responsibility and be assured that they can focus on the primary and not be overly distracted by the secondary (or tertiary, etc.).

A developer must be allowed to focus. It is well known amongst developers that a single quick phone call interruption can kill 20 minutes of effective development. An experienced developer who is focused can produce code rapidly and with few if any errors.

Developers are not QA level testers. There are a number of titles and labels for the various testing schemes at the various levels of development but developers generally perform unit tests on their code. Unit tests are fine but a number of development methods stress unit tests to the point that they should take up as much as half of the coding effort. The author takes the perspective that unit tests are appropriate for discrete modules that have testable components. However, not all parts of a project are easily unit tested with automated tools and spending too much time developing unit tests can be counter productive. It is a better use of resources to develop manual routines to test the code (arguably these could be considered manual unit tests). You can review **http://en.wikipedia.org/wiki/Unit_testing** for more details.

Quality Assurance (QA)

The QA team is generally the final authority on the quality of the project prior to release to the customer (the customer is always the final authority).

QA resources should be thought of much like valuable developers. Not doing so results in inexperienced and frustrated QA resources that tend to move between projects (or worse, jobs) and constantly need new training on the systems they are testing. They actually delay the development process rather than improve it.

Regardless of the development method used, the QA team should be involved from the beginning of the project. They can begin developing testing scenarios from the requirements and, working with the developers and analysts, adjust these as the project progresses. Some development methods insist that the QA person sit alongside the developers and client as code is developed. The author has not seen that as a particularly effective use of the QA resource. It is better that QA consult with the team as needed.

The QA team may have tools to test software, but much of the process is still manual and time should be generously allotted to testing.

There is some controversy as to the tools and techniques required to report bugs back to the developers. Some development methods insist that developers do not own the code and that anyone can work on anything. This often results in the QA team reporting bugs in a central database ordered by priority. In theory, the highest level bug is addressed by the first available developer.

In practice the author has not seen this to work effectively. Without ownership there is a tendency to not take responsibility. In addition, if the bug is unfamiliar to the developer in line to take on the bug fix, the time required to determine the issue and fix it is often far longer than for a developer who knows exactly what the bug report means.

However, the QA team may not know to what developer the bug should be assigned, or the QA team may assign it to the wrong developer. That developer must then spend time reviewing it and reassigning it to the proper developer.

Good personal communication with QA and developers as artists and development as craft will naturally address some of these vexing issue. QA will know better to whom to assign a bug and developers, out of personal pride, will take ownership and will attack a bug as soon as they identify it in the QA report.

Project Managers

There is an entire industry surrounding the project management profession. The author has yet to see an effective project manager.

The main problem the author has found with project management for software development is too little focus on resource loading, and too much focus on time lines and task definitions. Put bluntly, all of this is due to the common fact that project managers are clueless as to software development. Even if a project manager is a former developer, chances are their lead project manager (driving the staff project managers) is clueless.

We will not try and redefine project management in this report, however here are a few things to consider:

Understand the Full Time Equivalent (FTE) Resource

Project managers rarely understand what really is an FTE. An FTE is the work one person can do in one day. One day is commonly considered to be an eight hour work day. However, in practice no one works an effective full eight hours (sustainable over the long term) in one day. No matter how hard a person works, on average only about six effective hours are available in an eight hour day. Between breaks, meals, meetings, interruptions, the various crisis that pop up in every organization, vacations, sick, etc. even six hours a day is a highly effective resource.

When loading resources you should consider not work effort days (or units or other esoteric measurements), but work effort hours where six hours results in a scheduled day.

Properly load resources

Consider the common scenario in which a project manager consults with a development team on planning a project.

Resources will commonly double the amount of ideal work effort estimated for a task that they report to the project manager. Based on experience, resources know that nothing ever goes as planned and that padding is required to reach a true estimate.

The project manager will argue this estimate since the project has a fixed time line and some agreed upon estimate will be entered into the fixed schedule.

What then commonly occurs is the resources are overloaded due to both the altered estimates and the inevitable cramming of the entire project into the fixed schedule.

The author has seen project managers regularly overload resources to 200% and more. Often the project manager will not even consult the project resource reports to see the overloading. They simply throw resources at a task based on resource experience rather than availability.

Project managers should listen to the resources and use their estimates. If the project does not fit the fixed schedule then adjustments should be made. In no case should these adjustments create a resource overload. You can just about guarantee poor project results if resources are overloaded.

Trainers

Depending on the size and complexity of your project you may need a training team to educate the users on the new system.

Training and training techniques is an entire domain

in many companies and there is innumerable literature on the subject. If your company is large enough to have a training team, then take advantage of their services and incorporate them early into the project. Training departments often create and support the user documentation for a system. Again, take advantage of this if possible. Training should not write system documentation.

Image courtesy of Renjith Krishnan/FreeDigitalPhotos.net

Except for the smallest organizations, developers should not be trainers. Training is generally not in the developers experience domain and once the developer is presented (as teacher) to every user, the flood of support questions inevitably follows rendering the developer ineffective for development projects. If developers must be trainers then allot enough time and training for the developer so that their training of the users is successful. Then be sure and put the developer off limits to support questions.

Support

Except for small organizations you should have a dedicated support team. This team should be well trained (and rewarded) and be able to handle all but the most complex support incidents. You should rarely call in members of the development team on support calls. These are extremely distracting and time consuming to the development team. Too much involvement in support can bring other projects to a grinding halt.

The tools and techniques for recording support incidents is up to your organization, but it should not be so onerous as to be more effort than the actual incident support.

Management

Simply and bluntly put, management's role, like government's, should be to get out of the way of the people. Frankly management tends to micro-manage too much.

Like project management, there is an entire industry supporting management theory and tools, and obviously management needs to get involved in a project and make sure that the project managers keep the project on track. However, beyond the mandated HR roles, management's main role is to remove obstacles to the project and then stay out of the way.

How Should Teams be Formed?

It is recommended that management not force team composition. On the other hand, self organizing teams are inherently risky also. As such, you must strike a balance between the two.

Management, in cooperation with the potential team members must assess the project requirements and the expertise needed to meet the requirements. When this is complete the team will have a better understanding of the potential members that can fulfill the expertise requirements. You can then complete the team.

Be sure to consider the actual availability of the

potential members. A preferred member may not be available due to other commitments. Be sure to understand the resource loading of the project and other projects on which the members may be working.

Image courtesy of Renjith Krishnan/FreeDigitalPhotos.net

In addition, be sure to consider the extended members that may be required for the project but are not part of your resource pool of team members. This is regularly overlooked but is particularly critical in today's large project environments. Often extended team members are not even discovered until well into the project development phase. At this point it is a complete surprise to the extended team member that their expertise is required.

Who Manages the Team?

As recommended, management should generally take a hands-off approach to micro-managing a project. Teams of professionals, even as artists, should be able to accomplish a certain level of self management. Good project managers will also apply a certain level of management to a project as they enforce task and milestone completion.

However, in the event that a project gets off track it is important to asses why it is off track. Do not assume that people are not working hard enough or that you should throw more resources at the project.

Projects can get off track for a multitude of reasons, but reasons that often reoccur are:

Technical Difficulties

A technical issue resulting from a requirement is creating a roadblock of some type. The obvious solution is to analyze it and remove the roadblock. Be sure that the team is properly focused on the correct issue rather than simply a minor distraction issue.

Personality Difficulties

Teams members will have personal conflicts that impact projects. This is an HR related management issue and not a technical issue.

Resource Availability

Proper project and resource assessment will prevent most of these issues, but when it occurs it is usually related to an extended member/resource as described in team formation. Do your best to anticipate this and work with the management of the extended resource. It may take several layers of management to solve this.

Too Many Tools

Your resources should not be burdened by unproductive tool sets. A key issue of this type is project progress management. In other words, the process of reporting project progress is hindering the progress. Management likes project metrics such as burn rate, milestones, defect rates, etc. This is useful only to management so be sure that your

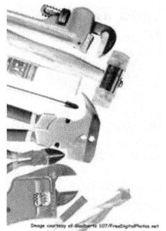

Image courtesy of Gualberto 107/FreeDigitalPhotos.net

reporting tools do not get in the way of the project.

In addition, developers have a tendency to want to use the latest and greatest tools and to follow the advise of respected gurus in the industry. This often creates an unending learning curve of new tools resulting in overall ineffective development. Stick to a limited number of proven tools.

When a project actually is off track then management must step in. In this case the main focus is not to assess blame but to remove roadblocks, offer alternatives (brainstorming with the team often results in self-resolving alternatives) and refocus the team on the project priorities.

Dump the Politics

Corporate politics (and gossip) have no business in the development process. Politics almost always result in a dispirited and unfocused team. One of a manager's key roles (related to removing road blocks) is to protect the team from politics.

This is not to say that managers should hide

information from the teams or lie in favor of project progress and efficiency. Rather managers should screen, filter and clarify the politics and gossip that naturally occur in organizations. This is a tough task as managers cannot know everything said in the work environment. A better approach is to be sure that the team members are secure enough to approach management with any concerns and when politics does rear its ugly head, be proactive and address it before it festers in the team ranks.

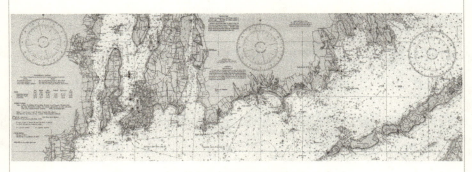

Conclusion

This executive report has provided the reader with the opinion of Jonathan Cook based on decades of experience in the field of Information Technology.

It provides insights and advice that in the opinion of Jonathan Cook will help you fine tune your processes by introducing elements and ideas often overlooked in the standard professional texts and consulting services.

After reading this text it is hoped that you will be able to find new ways to enhance your project management techniques and improve your results.

www.ingramcontent.com/pod-product-compliance
Lightning Source LLC
Chambersburg PA
CBHW051214050326
40689CB00008B/1302